Experiments with Water

By Angela Royston

Smart Apple Media

Published by Smart Apple Media,
an imprint of Black Rabbit Books
P.O. Box 3263, Mankato, Minnesota 56002
www.smartapplemedia.com

Cataloging-in-Publication Data is available from
the Library of Congress
ISBN: 978-1-62588-142-7 (library binding)
ISBN: 978-1-68071-014-4 (eBook)

Series editor: Sarah Peutrill
Art director: Jonathan Hair
Design: Matt Lilly and Ruth Walton
Consultant: Meredith Blakeney
Models: Rianna Aniakor, Dilvinder Dilan
Bhamra, Brandon Ford, India May Nugent

Credits: Igor Chaikovskiy/Shutterstock: 6b.
Johanna Goodyear/Shutterstock: 7c.
André Klassen/Shutterstock: 13b. NASA: 6t.
Matt Niebuhr/Shutterstock: 25b. Denis & Yulia
Pogostinis/Shutterstock: 7t.
Riekephotos/Shutterstock: 7b. Sue
Robinson/Shutterstock: 19b. Jurgen
Ziewe/Shutterstock: 11b.
Every attempt has been made
to clear copyright. Should there be any
inadvertent omission please apply to the
publisher for rectification.

Published by arrangement with Franklin Watts,
London.

Printed in the United States of America by CG
Book Printers, North Mankato, Minnesota.

PO1777
3-2016

Contents

Words in **bold** are in the glossary on pages 28–29.

What is Water?

Water is usually a clear liquid that falls from the sky as rain, flows along streams and rivers, and pours from taps. Water also exists as solid ice and as a gas, called water vapor.

Liquid water freezes into ice when its temperature drops below 32° F (0° C). As liquid water warms up, it slowly **evaporates**. It turns into water vapor. As the temperature rises, it evaporates faster. When it reaches 212° F (100° C), water **boils** and rapidly changes into water vapor.

▶ Most of the water in the world is in the seas and oceans, which cover 70 percent of the Earth.

▼ Thick ice covers the North and South Poles. Lumps of the ice break off and fall into the sea to form **icebergs** and **ice floes**.

Living things

Living things cannot survive without water. Plants take in water through their **roots**, while animals and humans drink it. Most food and all drinks, including milk, fruit juice, tea, and canned drinks, consist mainly of water.

People also use water to cook, to wash, and to clean clothes and other things.

◀ Plants need to be watered so that they will grow tall and healthy.

◀ This paper mill uses a huge amount of water to make paper from wood pulp.

▼ Dish soap is used along with water to clean dishes and other things.

The experiments in this book explore different aspects of water, such as how plants take in water, water as ice, and **surface tension**.

Coloring a White Flower

This experiment changes a white flower into a pink or blue flower. It also shows you how plants take in water.

You will need:
2 clear plastic
    cups of water
2 white flowers,
    such as tulips or
    carnations
Red and blue food
    coloring

1 Add red food coloring to one of the cups of water. Add blue food coloring to the other cup.

2 Put one flower into each cup and leave them overnight. Record what happens to the petals.

What happened?

Water evaporates from plants through tiny holes in their leaves and petals. To replace the water lost, the flower sucked in water through tiny tubes in its roots and stem. The petals are so thin you can see the colored water in them.

Multicolored Flower

If you feed a flower red and blue water, what color do you think the petals will go?

You will need:
A cup of red water
A cup of blue water
2 white flowers, such as tulips or carnations
Scissors

1 Ask an adult to split the stem of one of the flowers using scissors.

2 Put one half of the stem in the red water and the other half in the blue water. Leave the flower somewhere cool overnight. What do you think will happen?

3 Note what happens. Was your prediction right?

4 Repeat the experiment with the other flower, but this time leave the cup in a warm place such as a sunny windowsill or near a radiator. Does it speed up the process?

Popsicle Experiment

Make mini popsicles using an ice cube tray. At the same time conduct a scientific experiment to see what happens when water freezes.

You will need:
Water
Fruit syrup or
  fruit juice
Ice cube tray
Wooden sticks
Felt-tip pen
Jug

1 Add fruit syrup to the water, or use fruit juice. Pour the liquid into the ice cube tray. Do not fill the tray right to the top, but leave about 0.2 inches (5 mm) of space at the top.

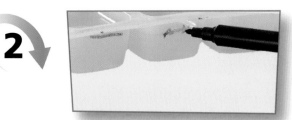

2 Put sticks into each compartment. Mark the level on the outside of the tray with a felt-tip pen.

3 Put the tray in the freezer. Leave for several hours, until the water has frozen.

4 When you take the ice cube tray out, check the height of the ice in the tray. Does the ice take up more or less space than the water did? Now you can enjoy the popsicles!

What happened?

Most liquids **contract** when they freeze, but water is unusual. It **expands** slightly as it freezes. This makes ice slightly lighter than the same **volume** of water, which is why ice floes and icebergs float. Drop an ice cube into a cup of water. Does the ice float?

▶ An iceberg floating in the Arctic Ocean. About one-seventh of the volume of the iceberg shows above the water. The rest is hidden below the surface.

The Ice and String Trick

In this experiment a piece of string cuts through a block of ice, but leaves it in one piece.

You will need:
A jug of water
A rectangular plastic box with a watertight lid
2 large plastic containers with handles, such as 1–gallon (4 liter) ice cream buckets

String, scissors, ruler
A bucket
Some weights such as potatoes
Two tables or chairs that are the same height

1 Fill the plastic box almost to the top with water. (Remember to leave space at the top.) Put on the lid and put the box in the freezer until the water freezes.

2 Fill the containers with the potatoes or similar weights. Cut about 16 inches (40 cm) of string and tie each end around the handle of a container.

3 Remove the block of ice from the box. If necessary, run warm water over the bottom of the box until the block slips out.

4 Balance the block of ice between the tables. Place the string over the ice so that the containers hang down on each side. Put a bucket underneath to catch the drips.

5 Check the ice about every 30 minutes. How long does it take for the string to pass through the ice?

What happened?

The weight of the containers caused the string to press down on a very small area of ice. The ice just below the string melted. As the string slowly moved down through the ice, the water above it refroze, leaving the block whole.

▶ Ice skaters glide on a thin film of water. The skater's weight pressing down on the narrow blade melts the ice below it.

Disappearing Salt

When you stir salt into water, the salt seems to disappear, but the water tastes salty. What has happened to the salt?

You will need:
A cup of warm water
1 teaspoon
Salt

1 Fill the cup half full with warm water and stir in a teaspoon of salt. The salt **dissolves** and disappears.

2 Add another teaspoon of salt, and stir. How many teaspoons of salt can you add before the salt no longer dissolves?

What happened?

The salt broke up into tiny pieces, which mixed into the water to make a **solution** of salt and water. The pieces of salt were too small to see, so the water looked clear. When water cannot hold any more salt, the solution is said to be **saturated**. The extra salt sinks to the bottom of the cup.

14

Soluble or Insoluble?

A solid that dissolves in a liquid is said to be soluble. If it does not dissolve, it is said to be insoluble. Test different **substances** to see if they are soluble or insoluble.

You will need:
A cup of water
A teaspoon
Sugar, sand, flour, soil, talcum powder

1 Test each substance one at a time. Which of them dissolves in water?

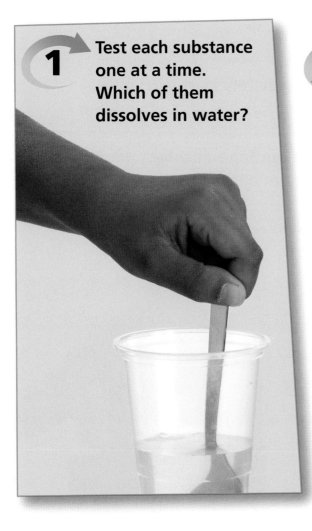

2 Make a chart to show which substances are soluble and which are insoluble.

substance	soluble	insoluble
talcum powder		
sand		
flour		
soil		
sugar		
?		

Do the soluble substances dissolve more easily in warm or cold water?

Growing Colored Crystals

Use a saturated solution to grow different colors of salt **crystals**.

You will need:
Boiling water
A plastic bowl
2 cups
Food coloring
A teaspoon
Salt
2 paperclips
2 pencils
String, scissors, ruler

1 Ask an adult to boil the water and pour about half a pitcher into the bowl.

2 Immediately start stirring in spoonfuls of salt. Keep adding salt until the solution is saturated and you can see salt collecting at the bottom of the bowl.

3 Pour the solution into the two cups. Add a few drops of different colored food coloring to each.

4 Cut two pieces of string about 5 inches (13 cm) long. Tie a paperclip to the end of each piece of string.

5 Balance a pencil across each cup. Tie the loose end of each string around a pencil so that the paperclip hangs in the solution.

6 Put the cups in a warm place. The crystals will start forming after several days.

What happened?

The water in the solution slowly evaporated and changed into water vapor. The remaining water could not hold as much salt, so some of the salt changed back into salt crystals. The crystals formed along the string and on the side of the cup.

Floating Pins

Solid metal sinks when you drop it into water. Or does it? Do you think a metal key, a pin, and a metal staple will float or sink?

You will need:
A plastic cup
of water
Small metal objects,
including a key,
a pin, and a paperclip

1 Drop the pin into the water with the point facing down. Does it float or sink?

2 Now dry the pin and lay it on top of the water lengthwise. Don't let the pin get wet. If you are very careful, the pin should lie on top of the surface.

18

3 Try to get the paperclip and the key to lie on the surface in the same way. Were you successful?

Repeat the experiment using salty water and water with sugar dissolved in it. Is the surface tension stronger now or weaker?

What happened?

Everything is made up of tiny particles called **molecules**. The molecules at the surface of the water clung together to form a kind of elastic skin, called surface tension. Surface tension in water is strong enough to support the weight of very light objects, such as the pin and the paperclip, but not a key.

◄ A pondskater walks across the surface of the water. It is so light it does not break the surface tension.

Scatter Shot

This experiment with surface tension has a surprising result.

You will need:
A bowl of water
Pepper
Dish soap

1 Sprinkle pepper over the surface of the water.

2 Squeeze a small squirt of dish soap into the center of the bowl. What happens to the pepper?

What happened?

The dish soap reduced the surface tension in the middle of the bowl. The molecules in the center were then pulled toward the edges of the bowl, where the surface tension was stronger. They shot outward, taking the grains of pepper with them.

Blowing Bubbles

Use soapy water and a loop of wire to blow bubbles. The soap reduces the surface tension of the water, allowing it to form a thin film around a bubble of air. The soapier the water, the larger the bubble!

You will need:
A cup of water
Dish soap
About 5 inches (13 cm) of wire

1 Add a large squirt of dish soap to the water.

Bend the wire to form a closed loop at one end.

2 Dip the loop into the cup so that a film of soapy water covers the loop.

3 Remove the loop from the cup. Blow gently.

How soap works

Soap works by reducing surface tension in the water. This allows the water to mix in with the dirt and wash it away. All kinds of soap work in the same way.

Bending a Spoon

Things often look different when you look at them through water. Water can make a spoon look bent, and it can make a hidden coin reappear.

1 Fill the glass half full with water.

2 Place the spoon in the glass of water. Now look at the glass and spoon from the side. Does the spoon look crooked?

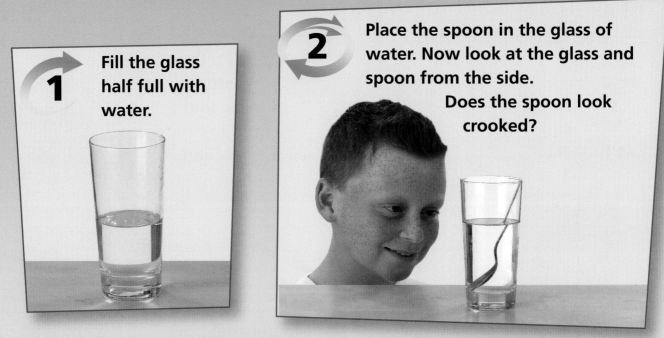

What happened?

Light always travels in straight lines. You see when light bounces off an object and travels into your eyes. The light from the bottom half of the spoon traveled through the water and then through air to reach your eyes. When light moves from one substance to another it changes direction so that the bottom half of the spoon no longer lines up with the top half. This is called **refraction**.

Seeing a Hidden Coin

You will need:
A bowl
A jug of water
A coin

1 Put the bowl on a table and place a coin in the bowl.

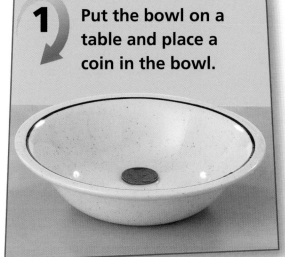

2 Move away from the table until the coin is just hidden below the rim of the bowl.

3 Ask a friend to fill the bowl with water. Can you see the coin now?

What happened?

Light from the coin bent as it traveled from the water into the air. This allowed you to see the hidden coin.

Make a Water Turbine

Using the power of flowing water is one of the cleanest ways to **generate** electricity. The water turns a **turbine**, a bit like the one in this experiment. Do this experiment outside or over a sink, and ask an adult to help you cut the bottle and make the holes.

You will need:
A jug of water
A large empty
  plastic bottle
Scissors
String
A ruler

1 Cut the top off the plastic bottle.

2 Make eight small holes with the point of the scissors evenly spaced around the bottom of the bottle.
Use the scissors to enlarge the holes into short slanted slits, all pointing upward at the same angle.

3 Make three holes evenly spaced around the top.

4 Cut two pieces of string each 8 inches (20 cm) long and one longer piece 16 inches (40 cm) long.

5 Thread each piece of string through a hole and knot it. Join the other end of the short strings to the longer string so that the bottle hangs straight.

6 Hold the end of the long string and pour water into the bottle. The bottle should spin around.

What happened?

The water rushed out of the slanted holes at an angle to the bottle. This pushed the bottle in the opposite direction from the flow of the water, making the bottle spin. In a hydroelectric power plant (right), the turbine spins very fast to generate electricity.

► The hydroelectric turbines are inside these huge cylinders.

Look—No Hands!

Can you hold a glass of water upside down without the water pouring out? Do this experiment over a bowl just in case it doesn't work!

You will need:
A glass of water
A piece of cardboard big enough to cover the mouth of the glass
A bowl

1 Fill the glass with water. Cover it with the cardboard.

2 Turn the glass and cardboard over, keeping the card pressed firmly against the glass.

What happened?

Air pushes in all directions, even upward. The force of the air pushing up on the cardboard was greater than the force of the water pushing downward, so the cardboard remained fixed to the glass.

3 Let go of the cardboard. What happens?

Hole in the Bottle

You will need:
Water
A plastic bottle with a lid
A sewing pin
A bowl

1 Fill the bottle up to the top with water. Screw the lid on tightly.

2 Use the sewing pin to make a small hole anywhere you like on the bottle. Does the water leak out?

3 Now, over a bowl or outside, take the top off. What happens?

What happened?

Air pressure pushing against the sides of the bottle stopped the water from flowing out. When you took the lid off, however, air pressure on the surface of the water, together with the weight of the water above the hole, forced water out through the hole.

Glossary

air pressure force produced by air pressing on something.

boils changes rapidly into a gas. When a liquid boils, bubbles of gas form in the liquid.

contract to become smaller in size.

crystal a regular solid with several flat surfaces and sharp angles.

dissolves breaks up into tiny pieces that mix into a liquid.

evaporates changes from a liquid to a gas.

expands becomes larger in size.

generate to produce.

iceberg a lump of ice made from fresh water that floats in the sea.

ice floe a lump of frozen, salty seawater.

molecule the smallest part of a substance that can exist by itself.

refraction the way light bends when it travels from one substance into another.

roots the parts of a plant that grow downward to take in water, which then moves up the stem to the rest of the plant.

saturated unable to hold any more.

solution a mixture made when a solid dissolves in a liquid.

substance the material that something is made of.

surface tension the force between the molecules of a liquid at the surface that produces a kind of weak skin.

turbine an engine that turns when water runs through it.

volume the amount of space that something takes up.

Further Information

Websites

ga.water.usgs.gov/edu/waterproperties.html
This website created by the US Geological Survey includes lots of facts about water and how it is supplied.

www.madsci.org/experiments/archive/854588066.Ph.html
How to make super bubbles using glycerine. Type experiments into "Search" at the bottom of the screen to get a list of other experiments on Mad Science.

www.water.epa.gov/learn/kids/drinkingwater/kids_k-3.cfm
This website created by the United States Government's Environmental Protection Agency includes information and games related to drinking water.

Note to parents and teachers: The publisher has made every effort to ensure that these websites are suitable for children. However, due to the nature of the Internet, we strongly advise the supervision of web access by a responsible adult.

Books

Junior Scientists: Experiment with Water by Charnan Simon and Ariel Kuzunas, Cherry Lake Publishing, 2010

Water (Explorer Library) by Charnan Simon, Cherry Lake Publishing, 2009

Water (Science Slam: Fun-Damental Experiments) by Ellen Lawrence, Bearport Publishing, 2013

Index